HOW TO LIVE BY FAITH IN A SECULAR WORLD

A Study of the Book of James

Written by
Rick White

Adult January Bible Study
LifeWay Press • Nashville, Tennessee

How to Become a Christian

ADMIT Admit to God that you are a sinner. Repent, turning away from your sin. Romans 3:23; 6:23, Acts 3:19; 1 John 1:9

BELIEVE By faith receive Jesus Christ as God's Son and accept Jesus' gift of forgiveness from sin. John 3:16; John 14:6; Acts 4:12; Romans 5:8; Ephesians 2:8-9; John 1:11-13

CONFESS Confess your faith in Jesus Christ as Savior and Lord. Romans 10:9-10,13

If you are choosing right now to believe Jesus died for your sins and to receive new life through Him, pray a prayer similar to this as you call upon Him alone to be your Savior and Lord:

Dear God, I know I am a sinner and have rebelled against you in many ways. I believe Jesus died for my sin and only through faith in His death and resurrection can I be forgiven. I now turn from my sin and ask Jesus to come into my life as my Savior and Lord. From this day forward, I will choose to follow Jesus and obey Him. Thank You, Lord Jesus, for loving me and for forgiving me. In Jesus name I pray.
Amen.

After you have received Jesus Christ into your life, share your decision with another person, and following Christ's example, ask for baptism by immersion in your local church as a public expression of your faith.
Romans 6:4; Colossians 2:6

Printed in the United States of America
© Copyright 2000 LifeWay Press
All rights reserved.
No part of this work may be reproduced or transmitted in any form or by any means, electronic or mechanical, including photocopying and recording, or by any information storage or retrieval system, except as may be expressly permitted in writing by the publisher. Requests for permission should be addressed in writing to LifeWay Press, 127 Ninth Avenue North, Nashville, TN 37234-0175.

This book is a resource for Developing Teaching Skills course (LS-0053) of the Leadership and Skill Development category in the Bible Studies subject area of the Christian Growth category (CG-0576) of the Christian Growth Study Plan.

Dewey Decimal Subject Heading:
Faith \ Christian Life \ Bible. New Testament: James—Study and Teaching
Dewey Decimal Classification Number: 241.4

ISBN: 0-6330-3537-8

HOW TO LIVE BY FAITH IN A SECULAR WORLD

A Study of the Book of James

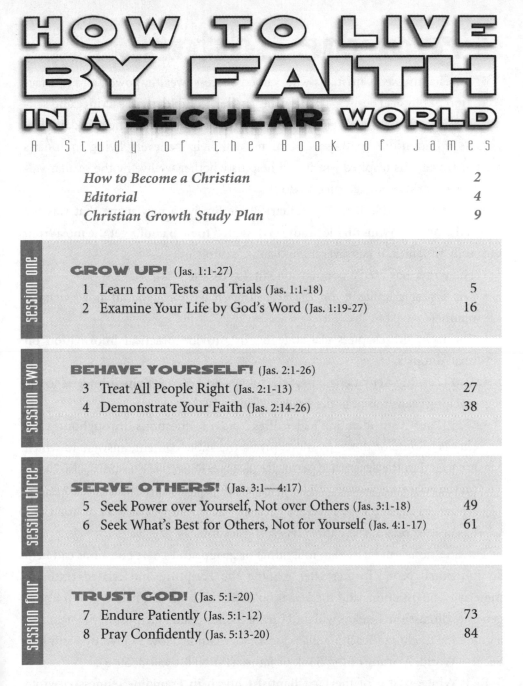

We believe the Bible has God for its author, salvation for its end, and truth, without any mixture of error, for its matter. The 1998 statement of *The Baptist Faith and Message* is our doctrinal guideline.

Unless otherwise indicated, Scripture quotations are from the NEW AMERICAN STANDARD BIBLE © copyright The Lockman Foundation, 1960, 1962, 1963, 1968, 1971, 1972, 1973, 1975, 1977, 1995. Used by permission.

From the Editor...

James addressed Christians who valued success, wealth, power, and satisfaction of physical desires. They saw little value in Bible study, sacrifice and self-denial, other people's rights and needs, or religion that affected daily life. James's admonitions to those Christians will help believers living in today's secular world. His inspired words will help us whether we live by the secular values of the world or are tempted to do so.

This Learner Guide for 2001 January Bible Study (a new name that was the original name for Winter Bible Study) is designed to help adults get the most from the study of James. It has several important features:

- The writer has used a popular style that is easy to read.
- The writer comments on the Scripture in a thorough but not extensive manner.
- Charts in the chapters elaborate on or provide practical information on related topics.
- Two Learning Activities are in each chapter, and each activity is integral to the teaching plans found in the Leader Guide.
- "For Your Consideration" identifies sets of questions throughout each chapter. Some of these questions probe the Bible content, answers to which are found in the designated Scripture passage. Reflective questions, also based on the Scripture passage, call for in-depth thought. Application questions lead readers to focus on the passage's present-day meaning. Each set of questions has at least one of these three types of questions.

The questions can be used in individual or group study. The questions can help an individual probe further after reading the Scripture and related textbook material. The questions and the Learning Activities both can help a group leader generate discussion. Leaders will find further commentary (Expository Notes) and a guide for teaching (Teaching Plans) in Leader Guide: How to Live By Faith in a Secular World: A Study of the Book of James (ISBN: 0-6330-3550-5).

Rick White, pastor of the First Baptist Church in Franklin, Tennessee, wrote these textbook chapters. Rick is an excellent communicator and presents the message of James in a clear and pointed manner.

Wayne Ozment

1

Learn from Tests and Trials

Scripture Verses   James 1:1-18

A company calls itself "No Bad Days Vacation Rentals." In an ad for one of their houses, they promise everything for a good vacation. They all but guarantee every vacation day there will be a great day.

The ad describes a million dollar view of the ocean, a swimming pool, four bedrooms including the master suite with the ocean view, a fully equipped kitchen, and a TV with a satellite dish that gets 30 channels of music. The ad also lists all kind of activities to enjoy. A vacationer can eat, play golf, and go fishing. There's also deep-sea diving, ocean cruises, and sightseeing or whale-watching boat tours. Or one can go parasailing, jet skiing, and shopping. What more could anyone want?

There is one other detail. The rates range from $1500 to $2800. The ad doesn't specify if that's per day or per week. Regardless, for most people such prices would ruin a vacation—every day there would be a bad day.

This company can't really live up to its name for most people. In fact, all of us have bad days. So the key is not how to avoid them but how to handle them. How do you handle a really bad day?

Problems Can Be Profitable (vv. 1-4)

Every day we face problems. Sometimes we see problems as something meant to hurt us. However, the Bible says our problems may be the tools God uses to bring about His purposes in our lives.

When you read a letter, you normally expect the author to warm up and then ease into the subject. You look for a few preliminary opening remarks before you get to the main message. But James dropped a bomb in verse 2: "Consider it all joy, my brethren, when you encounter various trials." How would you like to get a letter that begins like that?

Our problems may be the tools God uses to bring about His purposes in our lives.

©David Stoecklein/The Stock Market

For Your Consideration (1:1-4)

1. What progression of ideas did James use in moving from "various trials" to "lacking in nothing"? *testing faith*
   endurance
   perfect
   complete

2. What problem(s) are you facing now that could be an opportunity to grow in faith and wisdom?

3. Can you remember a time when you had greater spiritual endurance? What has changed?

Someone penned a positive little proverb: "When life hands you lemons, make lemonade." It's easy to say—catchy and positive—but it's quite difficult to live out. Most likely more of us identify with Shakespeare's words; we know about being "A man I am cross'd with adversity." Most of us would be surprised if we knew all of the hurts, pains, and bruises that are represented in our churches each Sunday.

Learning Activity 1

TEN THINGS TO TELL NEW CHRISTIANS

If I had only 10 things to tell new Christians, I would include the following as most important:

1. Stay in the Word

2. Don't give up

3. Be faithful in prayer

4. Be faithful in attending church

5. Expect difficulties hindrances

6. Family altar

7. Pray

8. Share witness with others

9. Learn to lean Christ

10. Nothing to separate from God

Accountability partner

James 1:1-4

Try to get people to do what is right & escape pain then receive blessings?

Am I following Jesus because I want to escape pain & be blessed

Love God

While some might suggest that adversity in life is evidence of some malady of faith, they draw that conclusion from outside Scripture. The Bible makes clear that problems have a purpose and add value to our lives. Verses 3-4 describe three purposes in the problems we face.

- *Problems test our faith.*—That's why James used the term "the testing of your faith" (v. 3). This truth was verified in the trials of Job. "But He knows the way I take; When He has tried me, I shall come forth as gold" (Job 23:10). Someone has said, "Christians are like tea bags. You don't know what's inside them until they are in hot water!"
- *Problems increase our endurance.*—When James wrote that "the testing of your faith produces endurance" (Jas. 1:3), he was referring to staying power. This is the ability to hang in there when we'd rather quit. We don't like pressure, but God will teach us to handle that pressure if we do not give up.
- *Problems refine our character.*—James called this the "perfect result" (v. 4) of our problems. God's ultimate purpose is for us to mature, to grow up, to think and act and react as Jesus did. Jesus faced the same kinds of problems that we do. Even a cursory look at the Gospels shows Jesus experienced loneliness, fatigue, temptation, and discouragement. As we go through what Jesus went through, God is working to make us like Jesus.

Why did James begin with "consider it all joy" (v. 2)? Because I can handle my problems when I choose a joyful attitude. A joyful attitude allows me to look ahead to the benefit this problem eventually will bring into my life. This is my choice. While I cannot choose my circumstances, neither Satan nor any person can take away my freedom to choose my attitude. I am comforted when I realize that.

Wisdom Is Available from God (vv. 5-8)

Life is full of decisions and that means evaluating, deciding, and drawing conclusions all the time. The quality of our lives is determined by the kind of decisions we make. Some we feel good about; some we later regret.

A young businesswoman went to her boss one day and asked, "What is the secret of business success?"

"Wise decisions," he replied.

"How can I learn to make wise decisions?" she asked.

"Experience," the CEO answered.

"How do I gain experience?"

"Dumb decisions!"

Praying when we have difficulty making a decision or when we face a problem is natural for us. But most of us pray for a quick end to the problem. James offered us an alternative. He said we should ask God for wisdom. Why? So we don't waste an opportunity to grow. If we are not paying attention to what God is teaching us in this situation, we face the possibility of being told, like the children of Israel, to take another lap around the desert!

1) disobedience

2) preparation for future ministry

3)

Learning Activity 2
GOD'S WISDOM

W

I

S

D

O

M

Characteristics of One...

Who is Double-minded   With God's Wisdom

For Your Consideration (1:5-8)

1. What is the role of faith in the midst of difficult circumstances?

2. What is the difference in human wisdom and God's wisdom?

3. How can Christians overcome being "double-minded" if they display such a characteristic?

Verse 8 reminds us of the danger of "being a double-minded" person who is "unstable." "Double-minded" means "pulled apart, divided loyalties, divided priorities." This term describes a Christian who wants his or her own will and God's at the same time. This kind of double-mindedness makes a believer unstable.

The only solution to this double-mindedness is wisdom. Wisdom is different from knowledge. Wisdom is making decisions about life based on the truth God has revealed to us in Scripture. It is knowledge put into practice. It is the ability to make decisions the way God would make those decisions. Thus to pray for wisdom is simply to pray for the ability to see all of life, and particularly our current

"Double-minded" means "pulled apart, divided loyalties, divided priorities."

©LeMay Photography

troublesome situation, from God's point of view. What a difference that change of perspective will bring!

Note that we aren't told to pray and ask God to make our decisions for us. Genesis 1 declares we are made in God's image. Part of that image is free will, the freedom to choose. God allows us to make our own decisions. But He doesn't leave us to make them alone.

IN DEPTH
Implications of "Double-mindedness"
- *Unstable in emotions.*—Not being able to make a decision creates stress. You can't sleep and you can't eat. You second-guess yourself. "Did I do the right thing?" The most miserable people on earth are the folks who are habitually indecisive.
- *Unstable in relationships.*—Lack of commitment destroys relationships. When you can't decide if you are going to stay or leave, you will destroy your marriage. When you are unstable in your commitment to your job, your employer can sense that and you will be the first to go when the next downsizing comes. When you are an indecisive parent, you raise confused, disobedient children. Relationships suffer when you cannot decide.
- *Unstable in spiritual lives.*—Verse 7 warns that the double-minded person should not expect anything from God. Double-mindedness leads to what I would call spiritual schizophrenia. It describes the Christian who sings "Onward Christian Soldiers" on Sunday but goes AWOL on Monday.

Prov. 10:22

Wisdom is ours for the asking (v. 5). Just as God was pleased to give wisdom to Solomon, God is pleased to give it to us as well. He also is pleased when we use that wisdom to make good decisions, especially in the midst of troublesome circumstances.

Do you see the pattern? Trials lead us to ask God for wisdom; then wisdom allows us to endure the problem until we are complete. Once again we see that the wisdom of God is *not* the wisdom of this world.

Priorities Need to Be Straight (vv. 9-12)

Interestingly, of all the areas James could have chosen to give as an example of where we need wisdom, he chose money. Why? More people make unwise decisions and foolish choices with their money than with almost anything else in the world.

When success comes our way, we often are tempted to believe it is a sign of God's blessing. James warned the

© Jonathan Nourok /Tony Stone Images

That many people make unwise decisions and foolish choices about money shows it is an area where we need wisdom.

rich person to remember how quickly wealth can be lost. Yet when we gain wisdom, we realize that wealth can become our source of security rather than God. We also note how seldom we experience significant spiritual growth in times of relative ease and prosperity. Whether rich or poor, all Christians will be subject to trials, all will have their faith tested, and all will arrive at heaven's gate with exactly the same amount of change in their pockets—$0.00!

For Your Consideration (1:9-12)

1. What spiritual benefits can you expect as you grow in perseverance in the midst of troubling circumstances?

2. Why do you think "flowering grass" is an appropriate symbol for those with wealth?

3. How has having or not having money influenced your spiritual growth? How has God used financial difficulty to draw you closer to Him?

Material resources will not get us through the tough times of life. Thus one example of wisdom is deciding not to spend a life accumulating what will let us down when we need help the most. Yet many people, even many Christians, give themselves over to the priority of pursuing wealth, much to the detriment of their character. God cannot build our character without our cooperation. We must surrender our wills to Him, give up control, give up our agenda. Then as we grow in character—as we grow in maturity—His priorities become our priorities.

2 Tim 6:19
Prov. 10:22

Temptation Can Be Overcome (vv. 13-18)

An exasperated man abandoned his car in a no-parking zone and left this note on the windshield: "I've circled this block 20 times. I have an appointment I must keep or lose my job. 'Forgive us our trespasses.'"

against lottery
Prov. 28:20

The man returned from his appointment and found a note from the traffic officer. It read: "I've circled this block for 20 years. If I don't give you a ticket, I'll lose my job. 'Lead us not into temptation.'"

good steward
time, money

Verses 13-18 give us a close look at a serious subject. The same Greek word can be translated both "trial" and "temptation." The context determines which definition is meant. When trials come from God, they help us grow up in our faith. When temptations come from Satan, they cause us to sin against God. Satan tempts us to bring out the worst in us; God tests us to bring out the best in us.

Tendency chart
Habit
Devil preys on our Tendency chart

Trials and tribulations are a part of life. When we complain about them, when we whine about the difficulties of living a Christian life in a secular society, we really are demonstrating spiritual immaturity. We are demonstrating we have bought into the lie that we should be exempt from problems, that "we are good people and deserve better."

IN DEPTH

Overcoming Temptation—Four Truths and Four Actions

- *Know the truth about sin.—* Verse 14 clearly states how sin happens. Our "own lust" drags us away from God's will. Verse 15 compares sin to a monster that appears harmless enough at first but when allowed to reach maturity, destroys us. The Bible teaches that we are all sinners by nature, that all sin can be forgiven, and that all sin has consequences. We also learn from this passage that God never tempts us. Instead God offers us a way out of any temptation we face if we will simply look for that way out. *The action step here is to be informed.*

- *Know the truth about temptation.—*Verse 13 assures us that temptation is a fact of life—none of us are exempt. James did not say, "If you are tempted." Rather he said, "When you are tempted. " Even Jesus faced temptation in the wilderness, yet He did not sin. While God can always provide us a way out, temptation is always easier to escape if we deal with it quickly, using the truths of the Word of God to refute Satan's lies. If we hesitate, if we procrastinate in resisting a particular temptation, it will quickly grow to appear irresistible. *The action step here is to be ready.*

- *Know the truth about yourself.—*Sometimes people fall into deep sin because they mistakenly believe, Oh, that could never happen to me. Each of us needs to recognize that we are just as capable of unspeakable evil as the worst adulterer or liar or serial killer. To believe otherwise is to deny what God's Word teaches in Jeremiah 17:9: "The heart is more deceitful than all else And is desperately sick; Who can understand it?" Coming to terms with our own capacity for sin causes us to quit blaming our parents, society, our spouse, the devil, even God for our actions. *The action step here is to be responsible.*

- *Know the truth about God.—*Verse 17 tells us that God is good and unchanging. He gives good things to us and does good things for us. God is always ready to forgive us no matter how miserably we have failed. Any unpleasant associations we may have had with the word Father need to be identified and rejected. Our Heavenly Father is good and giving and loving. *The action step is to be thankful.*

Maturity brings with it the realization that in trials we have opportunities to profit from our problems. With trials come opportunities to grow in wisdom. With trials come opportunities to realign our priorities. And with trials come opportunities to overcome temptation.

For Your Consideration (1:13-18)

1. What are both the short-term and long-term consequences of yielding to temptation?

2. Why is it so hard for us to believe that we are capable of committing evil?

3. To what degree are you successful in overcoming temptation? Why?

It should come as no surprise that temptation is rooted in deception. Satan is the master of the half-truth. Ultimately God's truth is our only defense against the deception of the enemy and the only way to win over temptation.

CHAPTER

Examine Your Life by God's Word

Scripture Verses	James 1:19-27

A missionary told about working in New Mexico several years ago. Once he took some Navajo children to see a movie, a western. A scene near the end portrayed Indians' surrendering to white men. The Indians spoke in Navajo but English subtitles translated their words as a beautiful speech of surrender and submission. The Navajo children laughed aloud. They knew the Indians had really said, "You white men are so low you can walk under a snake's belly and not knock off your tall hat." The subtitles had given the opposite meaning to their words!

When we translate the Bible through our lives, do we make it say what is written there? Or do our deeds mistranslate God's words?

James 1:19-27 is really about divorce, but not the kind that divides a husband and wife. It concerns the separation of action and attitude. It has nothing to do with incompatibility but rather with inconsistency. The Book of James speaks to the inconsistency in our faith between belief and behavior, between profession and performance.

The Bible remains a bestseller in the world today. In America Bibles are everywhere. But just because you have a Bible on your coffee table doesn't mean you will benefit from it. Application is not automatic. That's why we need to know not only how to read the Bible but also how to live life "by the Book."

IN DEPTH

Some General Observations About James 1:19-27

- This passage expresses imperative truth. These truths are to be taken as commands, "Know this!"
- These words express family truth. The frequent use of "brethren" directs these truths to all in the Christian community.
- These words express personal truth. Everyone in the church is to live individually by these truths.
- These words are logical truth. There is preparation, reception, and application in each phrase.

Prepare to Hear God's Word (vv. 19-21)

Notice the various commands in verses 19 21 related to preparing to hear the truth of God's Word. Preparation for any significant task is often harder and takes more time than the task itself. Whether you are painting a house, cooking a meal, or teaching a Bible study class, good preparation leads to long and lasting results. Nowhere is that more important than in the area of preparing to receive the Word of God. Here is a question that makes many of us squirm: How much of the Scripture you are exposed to really impacts your life?

For Your Consideration (1:19-21)

1. What instructions are found in verse 19 about preparing to hear God's Word?

2. How do the instructions in verse 19 relate to those in verse 21?

3. What attitudes and actions prohibit you from hearing God's Word to you? Consider carefully the possibilities of pride, self-reliance, lack of concern for the needy, anger, immorality, and others.

4. Think of times you have spoken too soon and regretted it. Compare that to the number of times you've wanted to speak harshly and withheld it. Which is the greater number? Why?

5. To which of the instructions in verse 19 have you paid little attention? Which of your relationships has that failure most affected? What will you do as a result?

Learning Activity 1

DO'S AND DON'TS

What are some actions that Scripture teaches you are to do?

What are some actions that Scripture teaches you are not to do?

Unlike one of our mirrors, which reflects only our outward appearance, the Word of God reveals our inner character.

©Kevin Hogan

While pastors and teachers have a responsibility to deliver the truth of God's Word, we all have the responsibility to prepare for receiving the truth. That preparation has to be both physical and spiritual. Many come to worship services or Bible study unprepared to hear and receive the Word.

In preparing to receive the truth we must be quick to hear and quick to listen. Hearing the Word with our ears is not enough; we also must be careful to listen with our hearts to what God is saying. A time for silence is needed in preparing to receive the Word. Learning to control our tongues and listening are essential to our growth and maturity.

Verses 19-20 remind us that we must be careful not to allow our tempers to flare, igniting an angry spirit. The Word of God cannot take root in a heart overrun with resentment and revenge. If we are going to mature in our faith, we have to deal with our anger. The Greek word used here indicates a long-standing resentment towards a person.

The application of this passage has significant implications for all the relationships in our lives. Conflict is too often the result of failing to listen carefully to others and of being too quick to speak and too quick to explode in anger. If husbands and wives, parents and children, employees and employers were all quick to listen, slow to speak, and slow to become angry, our lives would be much happier and more peaceful!

IN DEPTH
Old Testament Wisdom Echoed in James

- Proverbs 1:5–"A wise man will hear and increase in learning, And a man of understanding will acquire wise counsel." Be quick to listen.
- Proverbs 15:1–"A gentle answer turns away wrath, But a harsh word stirs up anger." Be slow to speak.
- Proverbs 29:11–"A fool always loses his temper, But a wise man holds it back." Be slow to anger.

To prepare ourselves to hear God's Word, we must first "put aside (literally "strip off" as we would a garment) "all filthiness and all that remains of wickedness." "Filthiness" can be used for the filth that soils clothes or the body. In a medical sense the Greek word means "wax in the ear." William Barclay says, "When wax gathers in the ear, it can make a man deaf; and a man's sins can make him deaf to God." The word translated "wickedness" often refers to hidden sins, motives, and attitudes that no one else sees. But God sees them. Therefore we prepare to receive the Word by coming clean with our sins. First John 1:9 says, "If we confess our sins, He is faithful and righteous to forgive us our sins and to cleanse us from all unrighteousness."

The second preparatory step is to "receive" the word of God. Verse 21 describes this as a two-part process related respectively to an attitude and an action.

- Have the right attitude. This is expressed in the word "humility," which means "with gentleness, openness, and having a teachable spirit."
- Carry out the right action. This is expressed in the word "receive," which means "to welcome." We are to receive the Word of God into our lives with generous hospitality. We are to welcome the Word in total subjection to God's purpose and with a willingness to learn from Him.

Learning Activity 2

EXPLAIN THESE TERMS

List words and phrases to explain each of the following terms from James 1:19-21. These terms help us understand actions to take in preparing to hear God's Word.

1) quick to hear

2) slow to speak

3) slow to anger

4) put aside filthiness

5) put aside all that remains of wickedness

6) in humility receive the word implanted

Respond to God's Word (vv. 22-27)

Just because we have been in church or Bible study and have heard the Word does not mean that in fact we are applying what we have heard. Simply agreeing with the Word does not mean we actually are doing the Word. This is where James addressed the gross inconsistency in the lives of many professed Christians. He did it by giving instruction, by illustrating the instruction, and by presenting a closing application.

1. The Instruction—Be Doers of the Word (v. 22)

The instruction is to be "doers of the word, and not merely hearers who delude themselves." We are warned here not to be deluded, or deceived. Satan is always trying to deceive us, which is one reason the Bible calls him a liar—in fact, the father of lies. It's bad to be deceived by Satan, but it's even sadder for a Christian to deceive himself or herself. Unfortunately many of us have been deceived into believing that reading the Bible is an end in itself.

For Your Consideration (1:22)

1. What contrasting words are used in verse 22?

2. How does being deluded lead to not doing what God's Word teaches?

3. If you had to justify your faith in a court of law, what evidence and witnesses could you produce?

James was calling for action once we have been exposed to Scripture. He said it is not enough to be simply a hearer, one who audits a course. Auditors may listen carefully and take good notes, but they have no assignments, tests, or responsibilities. Those who audit the faith are deluded about their faith. Authentic faith proves or validates itself by applying what is heard.

Which Bible passages trouble you the most? Some say it's the passages that are unclear. That's not my problem. My problem is just the opposite. I am bothered much more by verses that are clear!

2. The Illustration—Look in the Mirror (vv. 23-25)

James then used a vivid illustration. He compared God's Word to a mirror. But unlike a regular mirror, which is only able to reflect outward appearance, the Word reveals our inner character, who we really are. The difference between hearing and not doing God's Word is like the difference between looking in the mirror when you arise and not doing anything about what you see. Most people will look in a mirror each morning and make the necessary corrections before going out in public. The person who lives by the Book gives careful attention to the Scriptures, responds positively, applies what is heard, and enjoys personal fulfillment.

For Your Consideration (1:23-25)

1. What kind of comparison did James use about looking into mirrors?

   One looks then forgets
   One looks & changes

2. How would you explain the phrase "the perfect law, the law of liberty"?

3. Why don't more Christians spend time carefully searching in God's Word instead of just casually glancing at it?

Another point worth mentioning is that James called us to personal application. I've never looked into a mirror and seen someone else's reflection staring back at me. Yet how easy to open God's Word and think I see application for someone else's life. "I wish Bill would read this passage. He really needs it." The truth is: What I see addressed in the pages of Scripture is not someone else's disobedience but rather my own.

3. The Application—Practice What You Profess (vv. 26-27)

James gave some inescapable application in verses 26-27. <u>We are to practice what we preach</u>. James reminded us that talk is cheap. Actions speak louder than words when it comes to authentic faith. This in no way implies that being generous and compassionate is the way to salvation. But it does remind us that caring for those in need was Jesus' top priority. In the social hierarchy of the first century, widows and orphans were at the bottom of the list.

For Your Consideration (1:26-27)

1. How did James define genuine religion?

   Bridle tongue

   See after widows + orphans

2. Does this definition describe your life? Why?

3. What opportunities have you missed to demonstrate the reality of your faith? How can you find and use other opportunities to demonstrate the reality of your faith?

We begin the process of living by the Book when our speech is consistent with our beliefs. We grow in that process when our actions follow suit, when we are genuinely concerned about the needs of others. Then we demonstrate that reality when we retain our Christian distinctiveness (saltiness) in a fallen world.

The real test of our Christian faith is not how often we attend the services, how many notes we take, how much we listen to Christian music, or the thousand other things we do and say that (for many) define contemporary church life. The real test comes day by day as we live out our faith in a world that does not know Christ.

Living out that faith may begin with meeting physical needs of people who are in dire straits. But we must never forget that people's greatest needs are not physical but spiritual. So our task is to be out in the world, rubbing shoulders with the irreligious, looking for opportunities to meet their immediate needs so they will be open to the solution to their greatest need.

Recently someone sent an email to our church asking if a particular man was a member of our church. When informed that the man was part of our congregation, he sent us another message. Under the title, "Today I witnessed a Christian in action," he told a story of his interaction with this member.

"If you don't already have a church home, will you be my guest at First Baptist Church?"

He related that he'd been waiting for a large shipment that was several weeks late. The trucking company where our member worked was to make the delivery but was not responsible for the delay. Nonetheless, when the customer finally received the shipment, he was furious. He said, "I had made up my mind that someone was going to get a piece of my mind even before I met your member. I treated him extremely poorly, even though none of the problems were any of his doing. After I had finished complaining and criticizing (or at least paused a bit), he stated, 'If you don't already have a church home, I'd like you to be my guest at First Baptist Church.'

"This floored me. I instantly realized what a jerk I had been. I do already have a church home, which I attend regularly with my family, but I certainly didn't learn my attitude from my church or my family or from biblical examples.

"Needless to say I felt like dirt. I apologized but my after-the-fact apology could not possibly have made up for what I put your member through. Despite my attacks, however, he was helpful, positive, and Christlike. I have never seen anything like it. Some of the best people I have known would not have handled this situation with the attitude he expressed.

"I feel it is my responsibility to express my appreciation to your member for his example and for the lesson of the day, if not the lesson of a lifetime. Also I hope that others may also learn from my mistake. I want to express my apology to him along with my sincerest thanks for a much-needed lesson."

This Christian man is an excellent example of what Peter urged: "Keep your behavior excellent . . . so that in the thing in which they slander you as evildoers, they may because of your good deeds, as they observe them, glorify God" (1 Pet. 2:12).

CHAPTER

3

Treat All People Right

No one likes favoritism. We don't want others to play favorites against us, and it doesn't matter where we are or who we are.

A child doesn't want a teacher to play favorites among the students. A teacher doesn't want the principal to play favorites among the faculty.

An employee of a company doesn't want management to play favorites among the workers. A company executive doesn't want a supplier to play favorites among the competition.

A church member doesn't want someone on the church staff to play favorites among church people. A staff member doesn't want anyone in the church to play favorites among those on the church's payroll.

Yet all of us are tempted and sometimes do play favorites toward other people. God, however, doesn't play favorites; and He doesn't want Christian to play favorites.

The Principle: Don't Show Favoritism (vv. 1-4)

The Greek word for "favoritism" in verse 1 is a compound word that means "to receive" and "face." It literally means "to receive somebody's face." It describes a superficial evaluation of another based on how that person looks. The term used here is found in three other New Testament passages, each of which assures us God is not a respecter of persons. When He judges, He judges the heart, not outward appearances.

But we have a tendency to evaluate others based on appearance, which often means we discriminate against them. Beauty is everything in our world. If you're a cute kid, you've got it made. If you're plain, tough luck! We judge people on their appearance—how they look or how they dress.

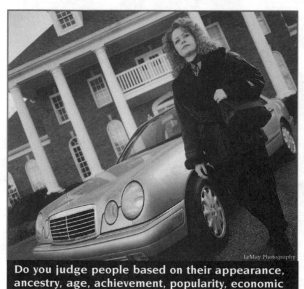

Do you judge people based on their appearance, ancestry, age, achievement, popularity, economic status?

We also judge people by their ancestry. We judge people according to their race, their nationality, their ethnic background. We judge them by their age—they're too young or too old. We judge people by their achievement. Our society gushes over a winner and forgets the loser. One minute he or she is a hero and the next minute a zero. Success and status are key words. I am deeply bothered by the increasing celebrity consciousness even in Christianity. The problem is this: Celebrities tend to expect special treatment.

For Your Consideration (2:1-4)

1. What example of showing favoritism did James give?

Rich over poor

2. Why do you think he chose this example?

3. Which of the following categories are you most likely to use to judge people? appearance? ancestry? age? achievement? popularity? economic status? Why?

James 2:1-4

Learning Activity 1

BRETHREN, WE HAVE MET TO WORSHIP

1. Brethren, we have met to worship And adore the Lord our God; / Will you pray with all your power, While we try to preach the Word? / All is vain unless the Spirit Of the Holy One comes down; / Brethren, pray, and holy manna Will be showered all around.

2. Brethren, see poor sinners round you Slumb'ring on the brink of woe; / Death is coming, hell is moving, Can you bear to let them go? / See our fathers and our mothers, And our children sinking down; / Brethren, pray, and holy manna Will be showered all around.

3. Sisters, will you join and help us? Moses' sister aided him; / Will you help the trembling mourners Who are struggling hard with sin? / Tell them all about the Savior, Tell them that He will be found; / Sisters, pray and holy manna Will be showered all around.

4. Let us love our God supremely, Let us love each other, too; / Let us love and pray for sinners, Till our God makes all things new. / Then He'll call us home to heaven, At His table we'll sit down; / Christ will gird Himself, and serve us With sweet manna all around.*

---

*Words by George Atkins. No. 379, "Brethren, We Have Met to Worship," *The Baptist Hymnal*, Convention Press, 1991.

The pastor of a large, prominent church told this story on himself: One spring evening he stopped by the church to encourage those who were there rehearsing for a musical presentation. He didn't intend to stay long, so he parked next to the entrance. After a few minutes he left and drove home.

The next morning he found a note in his office mailbox. It read: "A small thing, but Tuesday night when you came to rehearsal, you parked in the 'No Parking' area. A reaction from one of my crew (who did not recognize you until after you got out of the car) was, 'There's another jerk parking in the "No Parking" area!' We try hard not to allow people—even workers—to park anywhere other than the parking lots. I would appreciate your cooperation too." A member of the maintenance staff had signed the note.

The pastor said his estimation of this staff member went up because he had the courage to write a note calling his pastor to accountability. He acknowledged the staff member was right on the mark about him.

As he had driven up that night, he had thought, *I shouldn't park here, but after all, I am the pastor.* That translates: *I'm an exception to the rules.* But that employee wouldn't allow him to use that road.

The pastor admitted he is not the exception to church rules or to any of God's rules. As a leader, he's not to be an exception but an example. Scripture teaches that he is to live in such a way that he can say, "Follow me. Park where I park. Live as I live."

The pastor went on to declare that's why we all need people to hold us accountable for our actions. He concluded that staying in line on minor matters helps keep us from stumbling over larger ones. [1]

We also judge people by their economic status. James 2:2-4 specifies this as an area in which Christians discriminate. The passage describes an occasion when two men came into the assembly. One was obviously rich while the other was poor. One got the good seat; the other was offered a poor seat. Why? Because distinctions were made based on appearances. The motives were evil and selfish. The rich man was catered to with the hopes of selfish gain or to maintain class distinctions or simply out of pride and contempt. There is nothing inherently spiritual about being rich or poor. Both the rich and the poor are in need of Christ, and both have to deal with their attitudes toward money and other people.

The Problems with Favoritism (vv. 5-11)

If there is one place in the world where there shouldn't be any kind of discrimination, it ought to be the church. There is discrimination everywhere else in the world. But a church ought to be the one place where, no matter who you are or what your background is, you're welcomed.

If you want to be like Jesus, you can't play favorites. Romans 2:11 says, "For there is no partiality with God." Ephesians 6:9 says "And masters, do the same things to them, and give up threatening, knowing that both their Master and yours is in heaven, and there is no partiality with Him." Colossians 3:25 says, "For he who does wrong will receive the consequences of the wrong which he has done, and that without partiality."

1. Favoritism Is Unreasonable (vv. 5-7)

Everyone in America is rich compared to people in most of the world. Your economic status is of no importance to God. Wealth in itself does not mean you deserve any special treatment. Your value is not based on your valuables.

For Your Consideration (2:5-7)

1. Why did James indicate these Christians should not favor the wealthy? *Dishonored the poor & rich are ones who oppress*

2. In what sense did God choose the poor? *To be rich in faith*

3. Have you ever stereotyped people who make more or less money than you do? How?

Learning Activity 2

FIND A WORD PUZZLE

Find words that describe various sins of which a person may be guilty. The words listed below can be found forwards, backwards, from top to bottom, bottom to top, and diagonally.

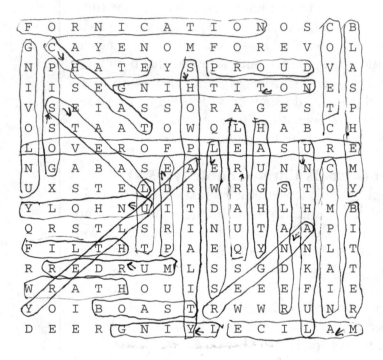

✓ Fornication	✓ Slander	✓ Proud
✓ Lying	✓ Hate	✓ Unholy
✓ Cheat	✓ Haughty	✓ Lust
✓ Boast	✓ Steal	✓ Lover of pleasure
✓ Gossip	✓ Anger	✓ Quarrel
✓ Murder	✓ Wrath	✓ Lewdness
✓ Covet	✓ Malice	✓ Pride
✓ Complain	✓ Blasphemy	✓ Adultery
✓ Unloving	✓ Filth	✓ Bitter ✓
✓ No tithing	✓ Unthankful	✓ Show partiality

Don't confuse your net worth with your self-worth. There's a big difference. Some people drive cars for transportation and others for status. Some wear a Rolex watch while others wear a Timex. Guess what? They both tell time. Your net worth and your self-worth have nothing to do with each other.

James wasn't trying to keep the rich out of the church. These verses show that the gospel is especially valuable to the poor, for it welcomes those who usually are not welcomed. Those who feel worthless in the eyes of the world discover they are valuable in the eyes of God.

In New Testament times the rich were persecuting Christians, judging Christians, insulting Christians, and blaspheming the name of Jesus. In essence James asked and told his readers, "Why are you worried about impressing such people? They're certainly not worried about impressing you. They're doing the opposite." God wants us to know that favoritism is unreasonable.

2. Favoritism Is Unloving (v. 8)

Verse 8 echoes what Jesus said in Matthew 22:39, "You shall love your neighbor as yourself." We can't get away from the fact that we need each other. Part of loving one another is acknowledging and being grateful for our interdependence. Thus favoritism is unloving.

For Your Consideration (2:8)

1. To what does "the royal law" refer?

scripture

2. Why is it called "the royal law"?

law of the King

3. What evidence is there that you observe this law?

A few years ago a heavy ice storm hit our part of the country. Many trees suffered fairly significant damage. Interestingly the trees with the worst damage were those that stood all alone. Where trees stood in groves, the branches and even the trunks of trees were leaning against each other, and that support often kept them from snapping off. When we play favorites, we are deliberately cutting some people off from the support they need and depriving ourselves of the support they might offer us.

3. Favoritism Is Unchristian (vv. 9-11)
We all have certain prejudices that affect our reactions and responses to people. Some hold prejudice against divorced people; or against those who have been emotionally ill; or against those who differ with them philosophically, politically, or even religiously. Such prejudice produces cliques, gossip, legalism, and power groups within a church. Certainly some sins are more heinous than others, but we're not any less guilty of breaking God's law simply because we only show partiality instead of committing murder. To show favoritism is to act in an unchristian manner toward others.

For Your Consideration (2:9-11)
1. How does verse 9 describe "partiality"?

2. Why is partiality described in this way?

3. Have you ever experienced discrimination because you were different? If so, how did that make you feel?

The Prescription for Avoiding Favoritism (vv. 12-13)
If favoritism is so wrong, how can we keep from showing it? Verses 12-13 give a two-part prescription to help us. If we'll keep both parts filled

James 2:9-12

and up-to-date, we can avoid favoritism.

Tress that stand all alone usually receive the worst damage in a storm.

The Stock Market

1. Live in Light of Judgment (v. 12)

Do you know why people have a hard time accepting others? They confuse acceptance with approval. You can accept another person without approving of his or her lifestyle. Such a one may be doing something totally contrary to the Word of God but you can accept him or her without approving of the sin that is involved.

For Your Consideration (2:12)

1. To what does the "law of liberty" refer?

2. What excuses do people make to justify excluding others?

3. How are you taking steps to create a more accepting environment in your church?

Some people won't like heaven because it's not exclusive enough. If we can't learn to get along together here on the earth, what makes us think we'll get along together in heaven? With some people we may have to use a little creativity to get along with them. We may have to look a little while. Maybe we just need to learn how to value some people for their uniqueness. Remembering that we'll be judged helps us accept others—and that helps us avoid favoritism.

What is God saying in James about our churches today? The church that accepts, appreciates, and affirms people is the church that God blesses. This behavior won't happen accidentally. It requires a deliberate effort by each member. Everybody contributes to the atmosphere of the church either negatively or positively. Would people come back to your church because of your warmth and acceptance?

2. Show Mercy (v. 13)

Prejudiced people are always judgmental. Those who have been set free by mercy should be the first to show mercy. Showing mercy will help us keep from playing favorites.

For Your Consideration (2:13)

1. What warning about judgment is found in verse 13?

2. How is being merciful to others related to not showing partiality to others? *mercy is seeking welfare of others at great cost to yourself*

3. What are you teaching children (yours or others) about loving people unconditionally?

His name was Bill. He had wild hair. He wore a T-shirt with holes in it, jeans, and no shoes. This was his wardrobe for his entire four years of college. He was kind of different but brilliant. He became a Christian while attending college.

James 2:13

Across the street from the campus was a church where everyone was well-dressed. One Sunday Bill decided to go there. He walked in wearing his usual wardrobe. The service had already begun as Bill started down the aisle looking for a seat. The auditorium was completely packed and he couldn't find a seat. Finally, he just sat down on the carpet near the front.

By now everyone was really uptight and the tension in the air was thick. From the back of the church, a deacon slowly began making his way toward Bill. A dignified, godly man, this deacon was in his 80s, with silver-gray hair and a three-piece suit. As he started toward the boy, everyone was thinking, *You can't blame him for asking the kid to leave. How could you expect a man of his age and background to understand some college kid who dresses like that and sits on the floor?*

The minister couldn't even preach his sermon because all the people were watching this man. As he reached Bill, he dropped his cane on the floor. With great difficulty he then lowered himself and sat down next to Bill.

When the minister gained control, he said, "What I'm about to preach, you will never remember. What you have just seen, you will never forget."

While we may be sensitive to sins of the flesh, sometimes we are very insensitive regarding sins of the spirit. Discrimination is a sin of the spirit that needs to be addressed in the life of every believer. Be careful how you live then. You may be the only Bible some people will ever read.

---

[1] Bill Hybels, "But I'm an Exception," *Leadership* (Spring 1988, vol. 9, No. 2), 37.

Demonstrate Your Faith

Scripture Verses	James 2:14-26

Our children used to sing what their teachers called an action song. Its verses begin with these lines:

If you're happy and you know it, clap your hands!
If you're happy and you know it, stomp your feet!
If you're happy and you know it, shout "hurray!"
If you're happy and you know it, do all three!

Each verse also has a line that reads "If you're happy and you know it, then your face will surely show it." A religious version of the song has a line that refers to showing you are saved by your life. There's some pretty good theology in those words. In fact they are exactly what James declared in the closing paragraph of chapter 2. Genuine faith produces genuine works. What art collector would rather have a bad copy than an original work of art? We're all interested in the real deal, the genuine article, the authentic original.

Faith and Inaction (vv. 14-17)

At first glance there seems to be an apparent contradiction between the theology of James and that of Paul. Paul emphasized that a person is justified by faith apart from the law. "For we maintain that a man is justified by faith apart from works of the Law" (Rom. 3:28).

James 2:14-17

Learning Activity 1

HYMNS OF FAITH

Locate hymn titles and text that help explain the meaning of genuine faith. List hymn titles and text in the space below.

What art collector would rather have a bad copy than an original work of art? We're all interested in the real deal, the genuine article, the authentic original.

© Kevin Hogan

In Ephesians 2:8-10 we read: "For by grace you have been saved through faith; and that not of yourselves, it is the gift of God; not as a result of works, so that no one may boast. For we are His workmanship, created in Christ Jesus for good works, which God prepared beforehand so that we would walk in them."

For Your Consideration (2:14-17)

1. What illustration did James use to show the relationship of faith and works? *need food & clothing - If we just talk about but don't do anything to help - won't do them any good*

2. How would you feel if you needed clothes or food and someone told you, "Go in peace, be warmed and be filled" but did nothing to meet your needs?

3. In what ways do your actions contradict your faith? How will you resolve these contradictions?

James declared "Even so faith, if it has no works, is dead, being by itself" (v. 17). In verse 24 he added that we are "justified by works and not by faith alone." For this reason Martin Luther labeled James an "epistle of straw." He believed it lacked solid, biblical doctrine. To Luther, whose battle cry in the Reformation was "justification by faith alone," the apparent battle cry of James, "justification by works," was blatant heresy.

It has been well said that Paul and James were not soldiers of different armies fighting against each other, but soldiers of the same army fighting back to back against enemies coming from opposite directions.[1]

IN DEPTH
The Theology of Paul and James

To understand there is no contradiction between James and Paul's theology, consider these three facts:

1. Paul emphasized the root of our salvation, while James focused on the fruit after salvation.
2. Paul looked at life from God's perspective, while James looked at life from a human perspective.
3. Paul used the term justification in reference to the act of God at salvation, while James used it to refer to validating or giving evidence of salvation.

"What use is it, my brethren," James asked, "if someone says he has faith but he has no works?" (v. 14). It's a rhetorical question. The obvious answer is: No use at all! "Can that faith save him?" Another rhetorical question. Again, the obvious answer: No! The words of 2 Corinthians 13:5-6 apply here: "Test yourselves to see if you are in the faith; examine yourselves! Or do you not recognize this about yourselves, that Jesus Christ is in you—unless indeed you fail the test? But I trust that you will realize that we ourselves do not fail the test."

We are saved by faith alone but not by faith that is alone. Genuine saving faith is accompanied by fruit; it is not found in the empty wastes of hollow words.

Learning Activity 2

HEROES OF FAITH

Read Hebrews 11 and identify some of the heroes of faith. List actions these persons did to demonstrate their faith. Compare these characteristics with those James identified.

Noah (Heb. 11:7)

Built ark as God warned him about things not yet seen

Abraham (Heb. 11:8-10)

Left home & went out not knowing where he was going but obeying God

Sarah (Heb. 11:11-12)

Had a child after child-bearing age God had promised her descendants

Moses (Heb. 11:23-29)

Left wealth & favored position to obey God — Kept the passover crossed Red Sea

Others (Heb. 11:32-38)

Gideon
BARAK
SAMSON
Jephthah
David
Samuel prophets

In Philippians Paul wrote: "So then, my beloved, just as you have always obeyed, not as in my presence only, but now much more in my absence, work out your salvation with fear and trembling; for it is God who is at work in you, both to will and to work for His good pleasure" (Phil. 2:12-13).

Real faith is not indifferent but rather is involved. Real faith is not indifferent to human needs but rather it is involved in meeting those needs. "If a brother or sister is without clothing and in need of daily food, and one of you says to them, 'Go in peace, be warmed and be filled,' and yet you do not give them what is necessary for their body, what use is that?" (Jas. 2:15-16).

The illustration in James is easy to understand because most of us have been there at one time or another. Warm, fuzzy, spiritual-sounding words won't get the job done when need is staring you in the face. An exhortation for a positive mental attitude during a time of personal crisis and need will not suffice. The proof of real faith in a situation like the one described in verses 15-16 is to provide real food and real clothes.

First John 3:17-18 says, "But whoever has the world's goods, and sees his brother in need and closes his heart against him, how does the love of God abide in him? Little children, let us not love with word or with tongue, but in deed and truth."

Faith was never meant to dwell alone, separate from the partner that proves its existence. Faith and works go together. An illustration of the balance between faith and works lies hidden within any tree. Leaves use up nutrients in the process of photosynthesis. As the leaves consume nutrients in the sap, suction is formed, which draws more sap from the roots. Without the sap, the leaves and branches would die. But the continual flow of this sap comes only as it is used up by the work of the leaf. Likewise, through faith we draw life from Christ. But a continual supply of fresh spiritual nutrients depends on our willingness to consume the old supply

A leaf draws its life from the nutrients in the tree's sap, and through faith we draw our spiritual life from Christ.

through our acts of obedience, through our works.

Real faith does not take place in isolation but in partnership with works. Thus James wrote "Faith, if it has no works, is dead, being by itself" (Jas. 2:17).

Faith and Action (vv. 18-20)

Real faith is not invisible; rather, it is placed on display (see v. 18). The word for "show" means "to bring to light, to display or exhibit." In the Sermon on the Mount Jesus commanded, "Let your light shine before men in such a way that they may see your good works, and glorify your Father who is in heaven" (Matt. 5:16).

For Your Consideration (2:18-20)

1. How did James show that genuine faith is more than believing in the existence of God?

2. What evidence do you have that you really belong to Christ?

3. Why are actions necessary for authentic faith? What does this tell you about the nature of faith?

James called for proof positive evidence of faith. He refused to allow us to back away in some corner and pronounce theological affirmations about our faith in God without validating those affirmations by our works and deeds of service in the kingdom.

Real faith is more than intellectual affirmation to theological truths. Real faith involves the faith commitment of the heart, That's why James said "the demons also believe" that God is one "and shudder" (Jas. 2:19). Even the demons have an orthodox belief, but they're still demons. A person may know factually all there is to know about Christ and still not be a genuine believer. James said that the demons shudder because of their belief. Some people don't even have that much response to the truth.

James was not demeaning an intelligent faith, but rather he was mocking those who always want to talk about the subject of faith but never demonstrate their faith is real or genuine. If we study verses 18-20 without giving consideration to application, then all we have done is gathered more information that is not going to make a difference in our lives.

Faith in Action (vv. 21-26)

As examples of faith in action, James called attention to two Old Testament personalities, Abraham and Rahab. Why these two people? Perhaps in order to highlight two different actions that validate faith.

1. Demonstrated by Obedience to God (vv. 21-24)

Abraham demonstrated his faith by his obedience. Specifically, Abraham did as God commanded and offered up Isaac as a sacrifice. That shows "faith was working with his works, and as a result of the works, faith was perfected" (v. 22). After referring to Genesis 15:6 and after describing Abraham as God's friend,

James concluded that we are "justified by works and not by faith alone" (v. 24).

For Your Consideration (2:21-24)
1. How did Abraham demonstrate genuine faith?

Obedience

2. How do you interpret the word "perfected"?

mature

3 How have you recently demonstrated your faith in Christ by obedience to God?

2. Demonstrated by Assistance to God's People (vv. 25-26)

Rahab demonstrated her faith when she risked her life to protect the two Israelite spies. She received the men from Joshua and helped them escape by leaving another way. Then James concluded that "just as the body without the spirit is dead, so also faith without works is dead" (v. 26).

There could hardly be two more different people than these two examples. One was a respected patriarch while the other was a pagan prostitute. Abraham was a moral, admired leader. Rahab was a harlot looked on with disrespect. However, both were justified, demonstrating their faith in the same way—by their action.

For Your Consideration (2:25-26)
1. How did Rahab demonstrate genuine faith?

James 2:21-26

2. Why do you think Rahab was selected as an example of one who demonstrated genuine faith?

3. How have you recently demonstrated your faith in Christ by assisting God's people?

Several years ago I saw a news report about a large group of skydivers. The photographer who filmed this jump was himself an experienced skydiver. He jumped from the plane along with numerous others in the group and filmed them as they floated through the air and then opened their parachutes.

Just as the final skydiver opened his parachute, the picture went berserk. The announcer then reported the cameraman had fallen to his death, having jumped out of the plane without his parachute. Only when he

Just as a spotlight reveals an actor's presence on a stage, so works reveal the presence of faith in a believer's life.

© LeMay Photography

reached for the absent rip cord did he realize he was free-falling without a parachute.

Until that point, the jump probably seemed exciting and fun. But tragically, he had acted with thoughtless haste and deadly foolishness. Nothing could save him, for his faith was in a parachute he had never buckled on.

Faith in anything but an all-sufficient God can be just as tragic spiritually. Only with faith in Jesus Christ dare we step into the dangerous excitement of life.

Someone who says, "I believe in Jesus!" needs to demonstrate his or her faith by action. Actions speak louder than words. Behavior shows what a person really believes.

What changes can I point to in my life? Is my lifestyle any different at all from nonbelievers? So many people think it doesn't matter what you do as long as you believe. James said that's not true. He did not say you can work your way to heaven. He did not say works deliver salvation. He did say works demonstrate salvation. He did ask, "If your faith doesn't work, what good is it?"

How do I know for sure that I am a Christian? you might ask. You settle it in your mind. Maybe you have had doubts about your salvation, your relationship with God. You're a good person and you've gone to church and maybe you've known about Christ and you've read the Bible and you've gone to Bible study classes. But are you absolutely sure that if you died today, you'd go to heaven? The fact is: You can be sure. If you haven't settled that issue, why not settle it today? (For help, see the article on p. 2.)

---

[1] Paraphrase of Alexander Ross, *The Epistles of James and John, The New International Commentary on the New Testament* (Grand Rapids: William B. Eerdmans Publishing Company, 1954), 53.

CHAPTER

2/9/01

Seek Power over Yourself, Not over Others

Scripture Verses	James 3:1-18

He was a heavyweight boxer who, just a few years ago, was considered a contender for the title. In each professional fight he grew in his ability to overpower his opponents. But his choices outside the boxing ring cut his career short. In 1996 he discovered he had contracted the HIV virus. Shortly thereafter he announced his retirement from boxing. He acknowledged his lifestyle had been wild and reckless and that it had included sexual promiscuity. He concluded that kind of lifestyle could have only one result: misery. Such is the legacy of those who never learn how to exert power over their sinful nature.

Beware of Seeking Control Through Teaching (vv. 1-2)
Some of us were born with a foot in our mouths—like the stock boy at the grocery store. A lady asked him, "Can I buy a half a lettuce?" He walked back to ask the manager, not realizing she was walking right behind him.

"You're not going to believe this, but there's an old bag out there who wants to buy half a head of lettuce." He turned around and saw her standing there and quickly added, "And this fine lady would like to buy the other half."

49

For Your Consideration (3:1-2)

1. What warning did James give to those who are or would be teachers?

2. Why are teachers held to such a high standard?

3. How can teachers' tongues get them in trouble?

Our mouths can get us into a lot of trouble. In essence James 3:2 reads, "If you can control your mouth, you're perfect." This doesn't refer to being sinless. The Greek word for "perfect" literally means "mature, healthy." When you go to the doctor and say, "I'm not feeling good," one of the first things he or she says is, "Stick out your tongue." Your tongue reveals what's going on inside of you, not just physically, but spiritually.

Because of this, James had warned the readers in verse 1 that stricter judgment will come to those who teach the Word. Teachers are required to teach the truth, not opinion. Just as important, they also are to live the truth they proclaim. Those who teach must live with their greater responsibility.

Be in Control of Your Speech (vv. 3-12)

Today is the information and communication age. You can talk with people all around the world in a matter of seconds. But did you ever wish you could take back something you said?

Most of us have multiple conversations each day and spend a large percent of our lives talking. That means we likely say thousands of words a day. It's hard for any of us to speak that much and still keep it all under control!

James warned that stricter judgment would come to those who teach the Word.

1. Because of Its Power (vv. 3-4)

Our words have tremendous influence and control over our lives. Where are you headed in life? Look at your conversation. What do you talk about the most? You shape your words and then your words shape you.

For Your Consideration (3:3-4)

1. To what did James compare a person's tongue?

2. Why do you think these comparisons are appropriate?

3. Is your speech under control or out of control? What changes do you need to make?

James said the tongue is small; it's tiny. Because it's tiny we may think it's insignificant. But it has tremendous power. This truth is illustrated by comparing the tongue to a horse's bit (v. 3). With that small piece of metal it is possible to control everything a horse does. You can take a 1,500 pound stallion with tremendous strength and speed, and yet a 95-pound weakling can control him with a small bar of metal placed strategically over his tongue. Likewise your tongue controls the direction of your life. It controls where you go; a little bit of a word or phrase can influence the total direction of your life.

A second illustration in James 3:4 compares the tongue to a ship's small rudder. The great sailing ships of the first century were dependent on strong winds for power but for direction they were dependent on "the inclination of the pilot" who controlled the rudder.

The Queen Mary has three anchors, each of which weighs the equivalent of 10 medium-sized cars. Yet a

Corel Photo Library

Your tongue is like a bit in a horse's mouth: though small, each can exercise surprising control over something much bigger.

relatively small rudder directs this huge ocean liner out in the middle of the waves and winds and seas, keeping it on course. The tongue is like that. Your tongue directs where you go. If you don't like the way you're life is headed right now, change the way you talk.

2. Because of Its Potential for Evil (vv. 5-8)

To show that our words have great potential for evil, James next compared the tongue to a small fire. A great forest can be "set aflame" by just a small fire (v. 5)!

In fact just one match can start a big fire. In 1983 in Australia, a fire destroyed miles of land, villages, and livestock across two states. All of this destruction started with a single match. Your tongue can destroy like that. A careless word can destroy a life or even thousands of lives overnight. I wonder how many people have destroyed their marriages or their careers or their reputations—or the reputation of another—or their churches or their friendships because of a careless word?

For Your Consideration (3:5-8)

1. To what did James compare a person's tongue?

fire

2. What are the long-term consequences of an undisciplined tongue?

3. How has your life been damaged by hurtful words from another? How have you damaged someone else by your words?

"Sticks and stones may break my bones, but names will never hurt me" is one of the great lies of childhood. Words do hurt. Fire (and words) under control can give tremendous warmth and light. But fire (and words) out of control can be devastating. Read verse 6 to find out how James saw the tongue's potential for evil.

We cannot tame our tongues. Only God can do that. To say our speech is "a restless evil" means it's always liable to break out at any moment. It's like poison. Just a few drops can kill.

Proverbs 21:23 in *The Living Bible* reads, "Keep your mouth closed and you'll stay out of trouble."[1] Pretty good advice!

3. Because of Its Possibilities (vv. 9-12)

James then carefully moved forward to show the tongue's possibilities. Our words reveal our real character. They tell what's really inside of us. The highest use of our mouths is singing or offering praise to the Lord. Then we walk out of church, get into the car, and on the way home we argue about where we're going to eat for lunch. One minute we're saying, "Praise the Lord." The next minute we're saying, "You're no good!"

Cursing here doesn't necessarily mean just profanity. It also means any sort of put-down or unkind label. Any put-down is cursing. Such is an affront to the God who made the person we're putting down.

Note the questions in verses 11-12. Whatever is in the well comes out in the water. Whatever is in the tree or vine comes out in the fruit. What is the likelihood of an apple tree producing cherries? None!

Learning Activity 1

THE TONGUE CAN BRING DESTRUCTION

List ways the tongue can bring destruction concerning:

1. Your Marriage or Family

2. Your Career

3. Your Reputation or Another Person's

4. Your Church

5. Your Friendships

6. Other Relationships or Areas

My mouth eventually betrays what is really inside me. I can fool you and pretend but eventually my tongue is going to catch me. My speech is going to let you know what's really inside.

A person who has a problem with his or her tongue in reality has a heart problem. A person with a harsh tongue has an angry heart. A person with a negative tongue has a fearful heart. A person with an overactive tongue has an unsettled heart. A person with a boasting tongue has an insecure heart. A person with a filthy tongue has an impure heart. A person who is critical all the time has a bitter heart.

On the other hand, a person who is always encouraging has a happy heart. A person who speaks gently has a loving heart. A person who speaks truthfully has an honest heart.

For Your Consideration (3:9-12)

1. What three illustrations did James use to show a Christian's speech should be consistent with his or her profession of faith?

   Fountain
   fig tree
   salt water

2. How can we bless God in our speech?

   praise

3. How consistent are your patterns of speech with your profession of faith? What changes will you make?

    What is the solution for those with a heart problem? Get a new heart. Jesus specializes in heart transplants.

Be Sure Godly Wisdom
Controls Your Conduct (vv. 13-17)

Every day we encounter different kinds of people. Some are delightful. Some are difficult. Some are inspiring. Some are irritating, fascinating, and intimidating.

© Bill Stormont/ The Stock Market

"The tongue...(can set) on fire the course of our life" (Jas. 3:6).

Learning Activity 2

CHARACTER TRAITS

List ways a person might demonstrate each of these character traits. Identify the short-term and long-term results of each trait.

A person with a harsh tongue and angry heart

isolation

Loneliness
cancer

A person with a negative tongue and fearful heart

depression

placing blame on others
low self-esteem

A person with an overactive tongue and unsettled heart

A person with a boasting tongue and insecure heart

A person with a filthy tongue and impure heart

A person who criticizes others from a bitter heart

A person who encourages others from a happy heart

A person with gentle speech and a loving heart

good listener
has friends

A person with truthful speech and an honest heart

The fact is, many of the problems we have in life are because of personality conflicts. We don't know how to get along with people. When our relationships are bad, everything about life is impacted. We may have lots of money and lots of opportunities, but if our relationships are bad, we're miserable. Learning how to apply wisdom in our relationships is very important.

1. When Godly Wisdom Is in Control (v. 13)

Did you know godly wisdom is available to help us control our speech as well as our actions? We need to be wise in how we act toward people. Often we treat people in foolish ways and we provoke the exact opposite behavior of what we would like to see in them.

For Your Consideration (3:13)
1. What actions demonstrate godly wisdom?

2. How does James's definition of "good behavior" compare with the usual definition of that term?

3. If someone had watched you for the last week, what evidence would they have that your behavior is controlled by godly wisdom?

Common sense is not so common. Wisdom is a way of living. It has nothing to do with our intelligence. It has everything to do with relationships and character. Godly wisdom is in control of us when we get along with other people. That shows how wise we really are. Wisdom has more to do with character in relationships than it has to do with education and intelligence.

2. Where Earthly Wisdom Leads (vv. 14-16)

James pulled no punches here. He described bitter jealousy, selfish ambition, arrogance, and lying against the truth as wisdom that does not come down from above. Instead it "is earthly, natural, demonic" (v. 15).

For Your Consideration (3:14-16)

1. As you read verse 14 and the list of the behaviors that characterizes false wisdom, which one makes you the most uncomfortable? Why?

2. Why are these behaviors described as "earthly, natural, demonic"?

3. In what ways have you reaped the consequences of trying to live by an earthly wisdom?

James used strong words to emphasize the insignificance of human wisdom. "Earthly" means this wisdom comes from the world and not from God "Natural" means it is not enlightened by the truth of the gospel. "Demonic" means it proceeds from an evil spirit or is demon-like." The end result of earthly wisdom is disorder, confusion, chaos, anarchy, and every evil practice, which includes all kinds of wickedness.

3. What Godly Wisdom Produces (v. 17)

Verse 17 is a descriptive list of the characteristics of the kind of wisdom that comes from God.

- Pure—sincere, moral, and having spiritual integrity.
- Peaceable—desiring, promoting, and being governed by peace.
- Gentle—fair, considerate; treats others with respect.
- Reasonable—approachable and willing to yield.
- Full of mercy—grants forgiveness to others.
- Unwavering—steadfast and impartial in treatment of others.
- Without hypocrisy—consistent and sincere.

Even a cursory comparison will convince us that God's wisdom is better than any we can conjure up ourselves!

For Your Consideration (3:17)

1. Which of these characteristics are present in your life? Which are absent?

2. How would you rank these characteristics beginning with the most important one?

3. How often do you demonstrate the kind of character that reveals God's wisdom in your life?

Be Assured You Will See Good Results (v. 18)

There is one positive result from applying God's wisdom in our lives: peace. It works itself out in two primary ways. One is in having a right relationship with God. The other is in having right relationships with others.

If you're at peace with others, you'll act wisely toward them. You won't rub it in when they are hurt—you will help them rub it out. You don't hold over their heads some hurt they've done to you—you forget it.

When somebody stumbles, you don't judge them—you encourage them. People don't need judgment when they stumble. They need encouragement. The wise thing is not to emphasize their mistake.

You sow in peace when you take kind actions toward others; it's something you do. You don't just show sympathy. You don't just say, "I feel for you, but you brought it all on yourself." You do something about it. You take action. You act kindly toward them. You demonstrate that you are a doer of the Word.

For Your Consideration (3:18)

1. What metaphor did James use to describe the results of having one's speech and conduct controlled by godly wisdom?

2. Why do you think "peace" is so prominent in this verse?

3. Are there broken relationships in your life right now? How does this passage encourage you to make them right?

James 2:13 reads, "Mercy triumphs over judgment." To show mercy is a greater principle than to offer judgment. If I'm wise, I won't emphasize your mistakes; I won't criticize your suggestions; I won't minimize your feelings; I won't antagonize you to anger; and I won't disguise my own weaknesses.

If I'm loving and wise, I'm going to make it in life. If you're loving and wise, you're going to make it in life.

As we saw in James 1:5, wisdom is a gift from God and He gives it generously to those who ask. Ask Him today. He loves to give.

---

¹Taken from *The Living Bible*. Copyright © Tyndall House Publishers, Wheaton, Illinois, 1971. Used by permission.

Seek What's Best for Others, Not for Yourself

Scripture Verses	James 4:1-17

Someone has said that the history of humanity can be traced more easily by its wars than by its accomplishments. That's sad but true. Even sadder is the parallel in biblical history. Conflict has always been a part of the community of faith:

- Lot could not get along with Abraham.
- Absalom led a rebellion against his father David.
- The disciples argued over greatness in the kingdom.
- The Corinthians were in conflict regarding spiritual gifts.
- The Galatians were warned about biting and devouring one another.
- The Ephesians had to be instructed regarding spiritual unity.
- Two women in the church at Philippi were told to live in harmony.
- Paul had a face-to-face confrontation with Peter.

In today's world some churches are better known for their internal debate than for their ministry in Christ's name. Following their human nature many in the church are producing a counterproductive message to the gospel. To some degree all of us are responsible for the damage that such does to the witness of the kingdom.

Eliminate Sources of Conflict (vv. 1-5)

"Among you" (v. 1) reminds us that all of James 4 refers to believers. "Quarrels" translates a Greek word used to describe the totality of war, such as the Vietnam War or World War II. "Conflicts" refers to specific battles within the larger war. James tackled head-on the internal problem among these early believers. He asked pointed questions, and then immediately plowed ahead to answer his own questions.

What are the "pleasures that wage war" among Christians? The Bible makes clear that there are three basic pleasures (desires) that can cause conflict. These desires are legitimate and God-given. However when they are out of control, trouble results.

1. *The desire to possess* (v. 2a).—According to Scripture God created all things for us to enjoy and use. We are to use things and love people. However sometimes the desire to possess can make us love things and use people. When we do that, conflict erupts. When we start loving things and using people, we can be assured our desire to possess is out of control. That's when we are guilty of lusting for things and of being envious of others who have those things. Possessions are never to be more important than relationships.

For Your Consideration (4:1-5)

1. What did James identify as "the source of quarrels and conflicts" among Christians?

   your pleasures

2. How many sins do you find referenced in these verses?

   lust   fight   altatuy
   murder   quarrel
   envy   ask w/ wrong motives
   *   pleasure*

3. Which of these sins have you committed?

4. For which of these sins have you yet to ask God's forgiveness?

5. How will eliminating selfishness from your life reduce conflict in your relationships?

2. *The desire for self-sufficiency* (vv. 2b,3).—James gave two reasons why our desires aren't fulfilled. First, we don't pray. Instead of looking to God, we look to other sources to fulfill our needs. Why don't we pray? Somehow we have convinced ourselves that we can be self-sufficient and that this is the way to live. We forget just how much we need God. If we really were more dependent on God and confessed our need for Him more, we'd pray more. We would experience less worry and more peace if we would pray more. The hymn writer put it this way:

> Oh, what peace we often forfeit,
> Oh, what needless pain we bear,
> All because we do not carry
> everything to God in prayer."

Second, when we do pray we often pray with the wrong motive. God has promised to meet all our needs. We have every right as His children to expect He will keep His promises and meet our needs. Unfortunately the line between genuine needs and self-gratifying wants is really blurred in our culture, even in the Christian culture.

Sometimes our motives in prayer have little if anything to do with what we need but are deeply anchored in selfishness. We want to feel good. We want to be comfortable. We want to have our senses satisfied. It's not wrong to enjoy life. But when pleasure becomes our number one goal, we are opening the door for conflict. How much conflict in the modern family can be traced to the pursuit of selfish pleasures?

3. *The desire for position* (vv. 4-5).—This passage describes those who are driven by a selfish and evil pride. They seek whatever will give them power, prominence, and popularity. They live by the motto, "I want to be number one." Their theme song, "I Did It My Way," summarizes their feelings.

We need to remember that the goal of the Christian life is not to see how close we can walk to the edge of the world and still be Christian. The goal is to see how close we can walk with God and how far we can stay away from the edge. Many adults accept the behavior of little children who do daring things to impress them and gain approval. God however does not approve close-to-the-edge behavior from His children. Such behavior is unacceptable for a mature, devoted follower of Christ.

Exhibit Humble Submission to God (vv. 6-12)

James also referred to conflict with God. Pride not only causes conflict in our relationships with other people but also in our relationship with God. Verse 6 says, "God is opposed to the proud." God declares war on selfishness. Have you noticed that God has a unique way of using the circumstances of life to deal with our pride? To be in opposition to God is dangerous. If we are legitimate children of the Father, He is going to deal with the issue of pride in our lives.

If pride is the source of conflicts in our relationships (both with God and with others), what is the cure? The cure is found in verses 6 and 10. "But He gives a greater grace. Therefore it says, 'God is opposed to the proud, but gives grace to the humble.' . . . Humble yourselves in the presence of the Lord, and He will exalt you."

Grace is how God acts toward people; He gives us what we do not deserve. When something about us needs changing, God will act on our behalf and use His power to change us. That's grace!

Do you know of anything in your life that needs to be changed so you can become more like God wants you to be? Whatever you would like to change will require something beyond your own power. What would you like to change about your relationships, your marriage, your family, or your friendships? Whatever comes to mind can be changed but only through God's power. You need God's power and that's what He offers out of His grace.

The only one way we can have an experience of God's grace is through humility. We must humble ourselves in the presence of the living God. He doesn't give grace to people who are full of pride and self-sufficiency. He wants us to confess, "God, I need your help." Then He will give us grace. He will work in our lives to make the changes we could not make.

The next few verses give five specific and practical actions to take in dealing with conflict. Remember, humility is the starting point. Here's how you diffuse conflict in any relationship.

Learning Activity 1

PRIDE AND HUMILITY

PRIDE	**HUMILITY**
Pride defined:	Humility defined:

PRIDE

Pride defined:

AN over high
opinion of oneself
exaggerated self-
estcem
haughtiness; arrogance
delight or satisfaction
in one's achievements

HUMILITY

Humility defined:

the state or
quality of being
humble of mind
or spirit
humble - having
or showing a
consciousness of
one's defects or
shortcomings

Examples of pride:

Examples of humility:

1. *Submit to God* (v. 7a).—Let God be God in your life. That's what "submit therefore to God" means. Give Him control. Quit trying to run your own life.

Verse 1 says "your pleasures . . . wage war in your members." Conflict with others is the result of conflict within. When you can't get along with other people, generally there is civil war going on inside you. This is the real issue. The starting point is getting peace inside before you can have peace outside. The real conflict is inside you. Who's in charge of your life?

The key to getting along with others is getting peace in our hearts through submitting to the rule of Christ. When we have the peace of Christ in our hearts, then we'll be at peace with other people. If we don't have this peace in our hearts, then we try to manipulate and control others so we can get our way.

2. *Resist the enemy* (v. 7b).—The Greek word for "resist" is a military term. It means "to take a stand against or to withstand an attack." The devil wants to destroy our relationships. He wants to destroy all the good things in life. Why? Because he is the author of confusion and conflict. He wants to cause disorder, arguments, stress, hurt feelings, disappointment, anger, chaos.

How does the devil operate? He plays on our pride, particularly wounded pride. He tells us what we want to hear. He whispers in our ear. He plants thoughts, suggestions, and ideas in our minds. In the middle of an argument we have all heard his voice: "You don't have to take this kind of stuff. Who do they think they are? Show them who they're trying to push around." He tells us all the things our pride loves to hear.

How do you resist the devil? The same way Jesus did it. He quoted Scripture. Proverbs 13:10 declares, "Pride leads to arguments."[1] The next time you get into an argument, this verse can be a vivid reminder to examine the issue of personal pride. Maybe there is something you are not willing to admit because your pride is too strong. James wrote, "Resist the devil and he will flee." We don't have to give in to the devil if we are wise about how he works and are willing to resist him.

For Your Consideration (4:6-12)

1. How many commands can you find in these verses?

Submit to God
Resist devil
Draw Near to God
Cleanse your hands
purify your hearts (mind)
Humble yourselves
Don't speak against brother
Don't judge

2. Which of these commands is the easiest to obey? Why?

3. Which of these commands is the most difficult to obey? Why?

4. Which of these commands do you obey?

5. Which of these commands do you need to start obeying?

6. How does submitting to the Lord's direction for your life allow you to seek what is best for others?

3. *Draw near to God* (v. 8a).—How does this Scripture help us eliminate conflict? Someone said long ago, the closer we get to God the farther away we realize we are and the farther away we get from God the less we realize we have moved from Him. Simply stated, the more time we spend alone with God, the better we get along with other people.

When we spend time with the Lord, we are better prepared to live in healthy relationships to others. If our attitudes towards Him are right, then our actions towards others seem to be right also. Of course some of us only draw close to God during times of trouble. Such people need to realize there is no substitute for a daily walk with God.

You will never be what God desires unless you spend time with Him. Find time, make time, schedule time every day to draw near to the Father. The conflict in your life may be in direct proportion to the time you're spending (or not spending) with God.

There is a great promise here too. When you draw close to God, He will come near to you. He will not back off.

When we spend time in the Lord, we are better prepared to live in healthy relationships with others.

4. *Cleanse your hands and purify your hearts* (vv. 8b,9).—If you want to stop the conflicts in your life, then you must learn to ask forgiveness from God and from those you hurt. "Hands" and "hearts" refer to actions and attitudes. Your hands represent your actions. Your hearts represent your attitudes. James was saying, "Clean up your act. "

Verse 9 goes on to tell us not to minimize the hurt in another person's life. Take it seriously. Be sorry for your self-centeredness. If someone says you've hurt them, you need to do something about it. It may not be a big deal to you but it is to them. Be willing to ask for their forgiveness.

Think of the person you are in conflict with right now. What would it take to resolve that conflict? Are you willing to apologize for your actions and attitudes? That will take humility! But remember, God gives grace to the humble!

If you want to change, that can happen in only one way—through an experience of God's grace. He will put His power to work in your life. That will release you to forgive and to be forgiven. This step is so hard that many who would really like to resolve conflicts just aren't willing to pay the price. Are you?

5. *Let God be the judge* (vv. 11-12).—Sometimes the most difficult sins we deal with are not sins of the flesh but sins of the spirit. When we judge

one another, we transgress the law of God. "To judge" means "to pronounce condemnation on someone." The only way we could judge another person correctly is to know everything about him or her. Judgment requires the kind of knowledge that only God possesses.

The reason we need to humble ourselves and be patient, forgive and show mercy is to follow Christ's example. Christ willingly humbled Himself so we might know God's patience, forgiveness, and mercy.

Emphasize God's Will (vv. 13-17)

Christians often talk about wanting to know the will of God for their lives. But for many there's a greater question, Would I do the will of God if He revealed it to me? Because they are afraid His will might be contrary to theirs, they plan their lives without Him. Verses 13-17 point out three mistakes people make regarding the future.

© Bruce Ayres /Tony Stone Images

When we judge one another, we transgress the law of God.

Learning Activity 2

GRACE AND PEACE

As the leader lectures, write words and phrases that describe *Grace:*

G

R

A

C

E

As the leader lectures, write words and phrases that describe *Peace:*

P

E

A

C

E

James 4:13-17

1. *We presume on tomorrow* (vv. 13-14).—Life is unpredictable. None of us knows what's going to happen tomorrow, much less next year. We presume on tomorrow in our finances and in our schedules. We make no place in our lives for God to do a new thing because we don't trust Him. Life is brief. We dare not take tomorrow for granted.

2. *We plan without God* (vv. 15-16).—The Bible teaches in Luke 14:28 that planning is a wise thing. But where does God enter your business plan? If you are a believer, your business is His business. Planning your future without God is practical atheism.

For Your Consideration (4:13-17)
1. To what did James compare his readers?

Vapor

© Chris Windsor/Tony Stone Images

Putting off doing the right thing is a trap.

71

2. What did James say about arrogance? Why do you think he added "all such boasting is evil"?

3. What are some evidences that you made your life plans through seeking God's will?

3. *We put off doing good* (v. 17).—This verse warns us about the sin of procrastination. James indicated that putting off doing the right thing leads to sins of omission. Most of us know the right thing to do, but that doesn't mean we're going to do it. Not doing what we know to be right is just as sinful as doing what we know to be wrong. Knowing God's will includes living obediently by faith and demonstrating our faith by the way we live.

---

¹Taken from *The Living Bible*. Copyright © Tyndall House Publishers, Wheaton, Illinois, 1971. Used by permission.

7

Endure Patiently

Scripture Verses	James 5:1-12

Endurance and patience are two words we hate to see in the same sentence. Endurance conjures up pictures of sweaty athletes grimacing in pain as they push toward the finish line. Patience is that virtue we all would like to have if we could find it on sale, but none of us want to pay full price for it! We know that patience can be acquired only during seasons of discomfort and even agony. Thus we often go out of our way to avoid those situations where patience could be a by-product.

It's little wonder that James addressed these two characteristics of a mature faith in this portion of his letter.

Endure Patiently Even Though
Some Misuse Wealth (vv. 1-6)

Few aspects of contemporary life are as potentially dangerous to our spiritual health as our relationship to money and the things it can buy. If we are to endure, we must recognize four common abuses of wealth.

Abuse number 1 is the accumulation of wealth (vv. 2-3). God is responsible for allowing us to make money in the first place. God says we aren't to stockpile money just for the sake of hoarding it. Verses 2-3 aren't a rebuke of savings, which obviously is a legitimate use of money. These verses refer to getting more and more simply for the sake of getting more and more.

In New Testament times those with wealth had a lot of food, clothes, and jewelry.

If you had wealth in New Testament times, you had a lot of food, clothes, and precious metals and jewels. These are probably the types of wealth James had in mind in verses 2-3.

Which clothes get moth eaten? The clothes you wear all the time or the ones hanging in the back of your closet that you never wear because you really don't need them? Which food goes bad? The food you eat every day for daily nutrition or the food that spoils because you have held on to it too long? The point is that everything we hoard deteriorates. So God desires for us to be careful about this matter of accumulation just for the sake of having more.

IN DEPTH
Five Important Truths About Money

1. Poverty is not inherently spiritual. Just as financial abundance is not necessarily evidence of God's blessing, neither is poverty a sign of spiritual maturity.
2. Wealth is not inherently evil. How we use our money determines the moral values we associate with it.
3. God's concern is not so much with our actual wealth as with our attitude toward wealth.
4. The danger we face is not in possessing riches but rather in riches possessing us.
5. We don't have to be rich to be possessed by riches.

Abuse number 2 is the appropriation of wealth (v. 4). God is not only concerned with what we have but also how we got it. There are a lot of different ways to make dishonest money.

Workers in the first century usually were hired at the beginning of the day for a day's work. They then received their pay at the end of the day.

Deut. 8:18

But there were no labor unions and few laws to protect workers. A person could work all day and go home empty-handed. The boss could say, "I don't like your work" and refuse to pay a worker. Some no doubt would call that "cutting down on operating expenses" but God calls it stealing. Being on the other end of such unfairness is common today. As companies "downsize" and "right-size" with only one goal, to squeeze as much money as possible out of the business, many employees find themselves being terminated with no just cause. We can survive such inequity only if we endure patiently, knowing that ultimately God's justice will be served.

For Your Consideration (5:1-6)

1. What misuses of wealth are described in this passage?

2. To how many of the misuses of wealth can you cite contemporary parallels? List them.

3. What are the consequences of misusing wealth?

4. Why do you think the name "Lord of Saboath" is significant?

The third abuse is the allocation of wealth (v. 5). Our society gets pleasure by watching people with money. We don't see many TV shows entitled "Lifestyles of the Poor and Unknown." However we are fascinated with the "Lifestyles of the Rich and Famous."

God is concerned not only with how we make money but also how we spend money. One of the greatest temptations we have to avoid as our income grows is the temptation to spend selfishly on ourselves. The more money we make, the easier it is to waste it. Our culture is constantly reinforcing the necessity of spending to bring personal pleasure. We tend to say things like, "I'm worth it. I can afford it, so why not?" Just because we can afford something does not mean we ought to buy it.

The fourth abuse is the application of wealth (v. 6). Wealth brings us much more than simply the ability to buy whatever we desire. We ought to recognize that money has a lot more power than simply buying power. Money gives us influence with others and sometimes places us in authority over them. Most of us are quick to listen to people who make more money than we do. We generally do not go seeking the advice and counsel of the poor.

Jesus said, "The sons of this age are more shrewd . . . than the sons of light" (Luke 16:8). The world recognizes that money means influence. Thus worldly people use it to influence others for personal reasons. While these reasons at times involve some good humanitarian cause, most of the time they involve personal greed. The use of wealth can be for motivation or manipulation.

Evidently in James's time the rich were buying off judges and circumventing justice. Today some still use money to manipulate others. I've known of families where one person would keep the relatives under control by threatening to cut them out of the will. This is the wrong application of wealth.

Christians ought to recognize the influence of money and use it for good. Believers are to use our affluence for good influence. We should recognize wealth is powerful and not abuse it. Then we can learn to use it in ways that build God's kingdom.

Hoarded wealth is going to decay and devalue. Those who are dishonest with regards to wealth, who waste it, and those who abuse

The "Lifestyles of the Rich and Famous" fascinate us.

© LeMay Photography

wealth will be judged in eternity. We ignore these words at our own spiritual peril.

Endure Patiently Because of the Lord's Coming (vv. 7-9)

We spend a lot of life just waiting. If you go to a restaurant, you wait for a table, wait for a menu, wait to order, wait for your food, and wait for your bill. Then you leave a sizable tip for someone often called a waiter.

In verses 1-6 James exposed and condemned the actions of the rich who were guilty of treating others with disregard. However beginning in verse 7 he turned his attention to the victims and exhorted them about a proper Christian response.

Three times verses 7-9 state or refer to the glorious truth that the Lord Jesus is coming back. That is the ultimate proof that God is in control of our world. God is in control of this world even when it seems the world is out of control. During the past couple of years we have lived and experienced horrible situations like Pearl, Jonesboro, Atlanta, Columbine, and Ft. Worth. These situations have made people ask, Who is in control?

For Your Consideration (5:7-9)

1. To what did James compare waiting for the Lord's coming?

2. Why do you think this is an accurate comparison?

3. How should the Lord's return bring hope and comfort and patience to those enduring hardship?

Be assured that God is in control and Christ is coming again. History is moving toward an honorable and victorious climax. God is in control of history because after all it is really "His story." He's got it all planned out; everything is on schedule; nothing is late; it's all moving in His perfect cadence. God's purpose for your life is greater than any problem you're facing right now. God is in control!

Learning Activity 1

ENDURE WITH PATIENCE

Following each situation listed, write a headline or a few words that describe a life situation related to that category. In the right column list ways a Christian can demonstrate patience in the midst of that situation knowing that Christ is coming again soon.

Situations we face   **Implications for Christians**

war/conflict

national crises

interpersonal strife

work or home conflicts

Have you figured out that a lot of life is beyond your control? James used a farmer as an example of one who lives with circumstances beyond his or her control. No one would try to go into farming without patience. If you have a lot of faith, you can be a farmer—but if not, you won't be able to farm.

Part of the job description of a farmer is waiting: waiting to till, waiting to plant, waiting to prune. These events cannot be rushed; the farmer can only wait for the appropriate time. There are so many factors over which the farmer has no control—weather, rain, heat, the economy, market prices, and good labor. Farming takes a lot of patience.

Though patient, farmers are still not idle. They are busy all year long—repairing or maintaining machinery, getting ready to plant or fertilize, applying weed control, and eventually harvesting. While they cannot manage the end results, they keep busy with the things they can manage.

We don't know when Jesus will return, but we know what to do until that time. He has given us the Great Commission and while we anticipate His coming, we have plenty to keep us busy!

We deal with a lot of other uncontrollable circumstances in life. Have you noticed that even when we realize a situation is beyond our control, we still try to control it? How? By worrying. We think that somehow worry will control a situation. To worry about something we can change is dumb. To worry about something we can't change is useless. Either way, we should not worry. We need to endure patiently in uncontrollable circumstances.

Endure Patiently Like
Old Testament Examples (vv. 10-11)

Though a situation may be out of our control, no circumstance is out of God's control. Although we can't control everything that happens in our lives, God can.

Learning Activity 2

EXAMPLES OF THE PROPHETS

Record responses based on the illustrated lecture by the leader. Then think of implications for Christians today based on the prophets' examples.

1. Elijah was ___threatened___ by Jezebel after he ___Rid___ the country of the prophets of Baal (1 Kings 19:1-4).

2. Jeremiah proclaimed that unless the people ___obeyed___, God would cause the temple to be destroyed. Those who heard his message, including the priests and false prophets, grabbed Jeremiah and ___seized___ ___him, saying You must die___ (Jer. 26:1-9).

3. Isaiah spoke boldly of judgment___coming___ including socioeconomic injustice, corruption of the legal system, the carousing of the rich, and spiritual insensitivity (Isa. 5:1-30).

4. The Lord announced to Ezekiel that his beloved wife was about to die suddenly. However, as an object lesson to Israel, the Lord commanded the prophet not to ___mourn___ over her death, as was the custom. Instead he could only ___groan silently___. He explained that they were not to mourn publicly over the ___destruction___ of their beloved city and its temple (Ezek. 24:15-27).

5. Daniel was thrown in a den of lions because he defied the king's law not to ___pray___ (Dan. 6).

6. The infidelity of Hosea's wife illustrated ___Israel infidelity___ even though God's faithful love was constant for them (Hos. 1—3).

7. God's call compelled Amos to preach so boldly ___about the death___ ___of exile___ of King Jeroboam and the upper class of Samaria that the prophet was ___to stop prophesying___ (Amos 7:7—8:2).

So we need to trust Him. Because God is in control and working everything out, we are to endure patiently.

God rewards patience. The second half of Job's life was more blessed than the first half. God doubled everything he had. There are all kinds of rewards for patience. The Book of James begins with the promise that "the testing of your faith produces endurance. And let endurance have its perfect result, so that you may be perfect and complete, lacking in nothing. . . . Blessed is a man who perseveres under trial; for once he has been approved, he will receive the crown of life which the Lord has promised to those who love Him" (1:3-4,12). Job's patient endurance provides another example of this biblical truth.

John 5:17

For Your Consideration (5:10-11)

1. To whom did James point as examples of patient endurance? To what other Bible characters could he have pointed?　*Job*

   Joseph, Moses, Noah

2. Who are some contemporary examples of patient endurance?

3. How is Job's eventual blessing evidence of God's compassion and mercy?

   God doubled everything he had

God was working all the time, even though Job had no idea what was happening. If you've been praying for an answer to prayer and you haven't received it, you may be tempted to think God doesn't want to give it to you. Remember, delay does not mean denial. Just as we teach our children, we have to learn the difference between "no" and "not yet." God is at work, even when we don't see what's going on. God was at work in Job's life, even while he was asking Why me?

God says, "Be patient because I'm working things out." While we are waiting, God is working. From our limited perspective the situation may be uncontrollable, but it is not uncontrollable from God's perspective.

Endure Patiently As You Speak (v. 12)

Does waiting ever tempt you to swear? While that is an inappropriate response to waiting, James had something else in mind here. He was referring instead to swearing an oath. In those days people commonly added an oath when making a pledge of any kind. This is similar to what witnesses do in a courtroom today: "I swear to tell the truth, the whole truth, and nothing but the truth, so help me God."

Swearing an oath in God's name was the highest guarantee anyone could make. People who wanted to be deceitful and dishonest often would swear instead by earth or by heaven. James wanted his readers to do better than that—to endure patiently.

For Your Consideration (5:12)

1. Of which teaching of Jesus does verse 12 remind you? Find and read it in your Bible.

2. Besides judgment, why did James condemn swearing "by heaven or by earth"?

3. How is not swearing related to enduring patiently?

4. How do you avoid swearing? What are some other secrets to not swearing?

Sometimes our impatience can lead us to say things that aren't true in an effort to ease the pressure we feel. A young mother was in the doctor's office with a sick child and noticed more than a dozen patients already sitting in the waiting room. "The doctor will be with you shortly," said the receptionist.

"Are all these people ahead of me?" she asked.

"Well, yes," the receptionist admitted. "The doctor was called to the hospital for an emergency."

"Then why did you tell me he'd be right with me?" the mother asked.

The receptionist thought a minute, then sheepishly replied, "I guess it's easier to say that than to tell the truth and have patients get mad at me."

We've all known the temptation to be less than truthful when we are in a difficult spot. James's admonition is to avoid that temptation and speak the truth, even if it adds to our difficulty.

Endure patiently. The benefits will be worth the effort.

Pray Confidently

Scripture Verses	James 5:13-20

I heard about a man who encountered a bit of trouble while flying his small plane. He called the control tower and said, "Pilot to tower, I'm 300 miles from the airport, 600 feet above the ground, and I'm out of fuel. I am descending rapidly. Please advise, Over."

Tower to pilot, "Repeat after me: 'Our Father who art in heaven.'"

You've seen it in the movies a hundred times. The doctor turns to the family in the waiting room and says, "I'm sorry, I've done everything I can. All I can do now is pray."

Where did we ever get the idea that prayer is only to be used as a last resort? At least seventy-five verses in the New Testament have something to say about prayer. Even the most casual reading of Scripture reveals that prayer was a major part of the life and ministry of Jesus and became the power source for those in the early church. Prayer is not a last resort but rather a first resource. Prayer is not a substitute for anything but preparation for everything.

Praying is mentioned seven times in James 5:13-20. Being able to talk to God is the greatest privilege of the Christian life. It also is the greatest source of power we have. We can pray to God about anything. But not praying is frequently our greatest failure in the Christian life. We talk a lot about prayer; we study about prayer; yet many of us are not satisfied with our prayer life.

Pray Confidently About Suffering (v. 13)

The Greek word for "suffer" literally means "to have hard experiences, to suffer misfortune." These experiences can include internal distress caused by an external circumstance. The circumstance may be a financial crisis, a relational crisis, or something else. It creates tension that goes to an all-time high and leaves a person heartbroken. Emotional hurts are just as real as physical hurts. The advice of James to those who are hurting: Pray!

But then James immediately referred to being cheerful and singing praises. Have you noticed that life is a series of pendulum swings from high to low, feast to famine, joy to problem? The Bible says, "Rejoice with those who rejoice and weep with those who weep." Both petition and praise are forms of prayer. The circumstances usually determine which we present to God first.

The word "suffer" in Greek literally means "to suffer misfortune, to be in distress."

For Your Consideration (5:13)

1. What two situations are mentioned in this verse? What two responses are encouraged? ~~Troubled — Happy~~

   ~~Prayer   Singing~~

2. Why do you think James called for the church to "sing praises" in response to a joyous situation?

3. In what ways are you suffering? In what ways are others suffering? How can prayer offer encouragement to you and others?

"Praise" is used over 400 times in the Bible. The lifestyle of the Christian is to be happy. If you want to know the secret of a rich, personal devotional life, trying singing. Nothing has done more for my own personal life than singing to the Lord. I sing a lot in my quiet time. One of our staff members uses the hymnal as part of his devotional life. I commend that practice to you also.

Pray Confidently About Sick People (vv. 14-15)

The lifestyle of a Christian is to be happy.

The word "sick" (v. 14) in Greek literally means "without strength." It describes a person who is totally wasted, fatigued, bedridden, and unable to work. This is a reference to a serious illness.

Verse 14 implies support for belonging to a local church. The church is a body and each of us are members of it. When we're sick or have some other need, we also have someone we can call on to help care for us. Thus this verse indicates the sick person initiates contact with the church.

For Your Consideration (5:14-15)

1. To whom are the sick directed to turn for help?

   Elders of the church

2. What is the your understanding of "anointing . . . with oil"?

3. How many times have you seen God answer a prayer for physical healing in a dramatic way? How does that bolster your faith?

Note the three instructions for the church's response. First is "anointing with . . . oil." This instruction may reflect a medicinal or a symbolic purpose. In the first century oil was known to have healing powers (see Luke 10:29-37). Oil also was known as a sign of answered prayer. Anointing believers assures them that God answers prayers of faith.

Second, do the anointing "in the name of the Lord." God is the healer, not any person. The name represents the character of the Lord. All healing is based on God's character.

Third, pray in faith. Verse 15 explains this in stating the results of praying for the sick and the basis for praying with great confidence. When we pray in faith we are assured that sick people will be healed and sins will be forgiven.

Why isn't everybody healed? I don't know. It is always in God's power to heal, but it is not always in God's purpose to heal. A clear example of this is Paul's experience, which he wrote about in 2 Corinthians. Paul prayed three times for God to heal a problem in his life, but three times God said, "No, I've got a better plan for you."

In our church we sometimes carry out James's instructions literally, but it is a low-key ministry. We just try to do what the Bible says. During an extended illness some of our people have called and someone on our staff has gone to their home, prayed for them, and anointed them with oil. It is always a powerful time of worship, and we always leave with a sense of awe at God's presence.

Pray Confidently About Sin and Forgiveness (v. 16)

In Jesus' day (and in some places today) it was taught that all sickness is a result of sin in a person's life. Jesus dismissed that idea in John 9 where He said about the man who had been born blind that no one sinned. We live in a fallen world and hurt and problems are the inevitable results.

On the other hand, we certainly do bring on a lot of sickness in our lives. If I don't follow God's principles for eating, sleeping, and exercising properly, then all kinds of ailments will come on me. I need to listen to God's Word about not being anxious about anything but praying about everything. If I don't and get an ulcer from my worry, then I'm to blame for it. If I allow resentment to build up in my life, it will take a physical toll.

For Your Consideration (5:16)

1. What affirmation of prayer is found in this verse?

Confess sins to each other

2. Why do you think confessing sins to God is not mentioned?

3. What are some instances in which confessing sins to another Christian might be helpful?

4. What guidelines will help ensure what you confess to others is appropriate?

What's the condition for healing in such cases? Confession. We'd prefer to conceal and camouflage our sins rather than confess them. To confess our sins is a liberating experience. We get them out and share them, not just with the Lord but with others. Someone has said, "Revealing your feeling is the beginning of healing."

People often say to me, "I've never told this to anyone else in the world." Once they say that, I know that something great is going to happen. They're going to feel the relief that follows from no longer having to carry a burden. They get it out and share it with somebody else.

Some are frightened by the phrase "confess to each other." Does that mean I get up and confess to the whole church? There is a principle called the circle of confession that says, "Only confess as widely as it involves other people." If I have a private sin, one that's between just the Lord and me, then I ought to confess it just to the Lord. If it's a personal sin, between you and me, then I need to come to you. If it's a public sin, then I need to apologize to the whole church. James said confess your sins, not broadcast them.

When should you pray? James said you can pray whenever you have a need—a physical need, an emotional need, a material need. Whatever the need, prayer is always appropriate.

Pray Confidently About Other Situations (vv. 17-18)

Some people think you have to be a spiritual giant to pray and get answers that involve a miracle. They say, "I could never pray and see somebody healed" or "I could never pray and see a financial miracle." Such Christians feel inferior.

For Your Consideration (5:17-18)

1. How did James characterize Elijah and his prayer life? *Just like us – prayed earnestly*

Learning Activity 1

COMPARE YOURSELF TO ELIJAH

Bible passages	Characteristics of Elijah	How you demonstrate these characteristics
1 Kings 17:1	Bold, trusted God	
1 Kings 18:36-37	Confident in God	
1 Kings 18:43-44	Persistent	
1 Kings 19:2-3	Fearful	
1 Kings 19:4	Worried, Depressed	
1 Kings 19:10	Lonely, Angry, Resentful	

2. Why is Elijah a good example of praying with confidence?

3. How would James characterize your prayer life?

For them, James used Elijah as an illustration. Elijah prayed earnestly that it wouldn't rain and it didn't rain on the land for three and a half years. He prayed again and the heavens gave rain and the earth produced its crops (1 Kings 18). This was after the "big god" contest on Mount Carmel. Elijah ran to the other side of the desert and went through a fit of depression and asked God to take his life (1 Kings 19). Elijah wasn't afraid of 400 prophets of Baal but he ran from a woman named Jezebel. Elijah demonstrated fear, resentment, guilt, anger, loneliness, and worry. Now you know why James stated that Elijah was a man just like us. We also have anger, fear, resentment, worry, and loneliness.

The lesson of Elijah's life is this: You don't have to be perfect to pray. You don't have to be perfect to see answers to your prayers. Prayer is for ordinary people. First Kings 18 tells of Elijah's humbling himself before God and praying for rain. He prayed seven times. He was persistent. He would not give up. One day a little cloud formed in the sky and he said, "It's going to be a gusher!" The rains came and flooded the place. God works through the prayers of ordinary people to do extraordinary things.

Pray Confidently About Those Who Stray (vv. 19-20)

James 5:19-20 makes clear that prodigals matter to God. That means they should matter to us. Restoration is an essential part of life in the body of Christ but many Christians are reluctant to be a part of the process.

Why are we so reluctant to make the effort to restore a brother or sister who is falling away from their faith? Part of that reluctance is a cultural influence that tells us, "Mind your own business—who do you think you are to correct someone else?" Add to that the general lack of accountability we have to one another, along with the false belief that religious faith is a private matter, and you can understand why such reluctance exists.

The lesson of Elijah's life is this: You don't have to be perfect to pray.

© 1993 Convention Press

For Your Consideration (5:19-20)

1. What are the results of turning "a sinner from . . . error"? How do you understand these results?

SAVE him from death
+ cover a multitude of sins

2. Why do you think these verses are included with a passage related to prayer?

3. Who are some Christians you know who have wandered from the faith? What are you willing to do to turn them back?

But more than anything, we lack an understanding of the biblical mandate to seek to restore one another. Ezekiel 34:16 says, "I will seek the lost, bring back the scattered, bind up the broken and strengthen the sick." Jesus said in Luke 17:3 "'Be on your guard! If your brother sins, rebuke him; and if he repents, forgive him.'" Paul told the young pastor Timothy to "preach the word; be ready in season and out of season; reprove, rebuke, exhort, with great patience and instruction" (2 Tim. 4:2).

Our motive must be one of love and concern and obedience, not a desire to hurt or humiliate. We must never consider ourselves to be above rebuke or our efforts to restore the wandering brother or sister will be lost. Most of all, we'll miss the significant spiritual rewards associated with bringing them home.

The Book of James has been a difficult study at times, but profitable. We've learned about the effect our faith has on our attitude during trials and tough situations. We've been instructed on how authentic faith affects our relationships. We've looked at the difference between authentic faith and the counterfeit that listens to God's Word but fails to act on it. We've been confronted with the importance of keeping a tight rein on our tongues. We've had to examine the motives within us that cause so much of the hurt and pain in our lives. We've been warned about pride, greed, and impatience.

And we've been challenged with the reality that prayer is not the last resort—it is the most significant thing we can do for one another as we strive toward living by faith in a secular world.

I pray that this study has raised the right questions in your mind. Is your lifestyle consistent with what James has taught about authentic Christianity? Is your faith a faith that works? Is your faith strong and practical enough to help you live effectively in an increasingly secular world? Is your faith and lifestyle based on Christian values or on the values of a secular world? In just 108 verses, we have been challenged in just about every area of life. What new ways have you discovered to integrate your faith into your work, your family, and your social relationships?

Learning Activity 2

A SUMMARY OF TEACHING IN JAMES

List at least one way to apply the lessons you discovered from the teaching of James.

James 1:1-18   Learn from Tests and Trials

James 1:19-27 Examine Your Life by God's Word

James 2:1-13   Treat All People Right

James 2:14-26 Demonstrate Your Faith

James 3:1-18   Seek Power over Yourself, Not over Others

James 4:1-17   Seek What's Best for Others, Not for Yourself

James 5:1-12   Endure Patiently

James 5:13-20 Pray Confidently

CHRISTIAN GROWTH STUDY PLAN

Preparing Christians to Serve

In the **Christian Growth Study Plan (formerly Church Study Course)**, this book *How to Live by Faith in a Secular World: A Study of the Book of James* is a resource for course credit in one **Leadership and Skill Development** diploma and two **Christian Growth** diploma plans.

To receive credit, read the book, complete the learning activities, show your work to your pastor, a staff member or church leader; then complete the information on the next page. The form may be duplicated. **Send the completed page to:**

Christian Growth Study Plan
127 Ninth Avenue, North
Nashville, TN 37234-0117
FAX: (615) 251-5067

For information about the Christian Growth Study Plan, refer to the current Christian Growth Study Plan Catalog. Your church office may have a copy. If not, request a free copy from the Christian Growth Study Plan office (615/251-2525).